Contents

Introduction
to Course & Subjects

This is a four part course designed to help participants learn more about their faith and how to apply it to everyday life, how to study the Bible and explore theology and become more effective leaders.

The subjects and some of the elements covered are:

Bible: Jesus, The Bible & You –
* How to read the Bible devotionally and for study purposes
* Historical background to the Bible
* How to use all the Bible study tools
* How to get revelations from the Bible

Leadership: The Church & Your Leadership Journey – Learn effective leadership qualities and skills that can build your own life and the lives of others, seeing the kingdom of God move forward.

Lifestyle: Following Jesus –
* How to build a strong devotional life
* How to find your purpose in God
* How to live a life that can fulfil your purpose
* How to hear from God

Theology: Faith Foundations – Develop a personal theology in a biblical and thoughtful way that will be a blessing to you and your church community.

Learning Sessions

Once per week for 2½ hours which includes 2 teaching sessions, 1 application session and a 20min break (after session 1).

Teaching Sessions – each week will include 2 x 50 minute sessions in a lecture style.

Application Sessions – each week will consist of 1 x 25 minute group session where homework and previous teaching sessions will be used to stimulate discussion. These sessions will vary in activities including multimedia and role playing etc.

Homework

Each week you will get a small amount of work to complete at home. It should take about 20 minutes to complete and it will be used to stimulate discussion the following week during the group session. There are also some advanced questions for those who wish to do more in-depth study.

Bible Version

Throughout this course the New International Version (NIV) has been used unless otherwise specified.

Many translations can be viewed freely from websites such as: **www.biblegateway.com**, **www.biblestudytools.com** and **www.bible.cc** or on your mobile device using applications such as **YouVersion**. We encourage you to research and find what works best for you.

Before you commence spend a few moments to pray and ask the Holy Spirit to give you eyes to see what the Word is saying to you.

Theology
Faith Foundations

This subject gives a seven-week overview of what Theology is, why it is important and how it is relevant and outworked in your local church today.

Recommend Reading

If you want to get a deeper understanding of this subject, here are some recommended resources:

* Millard J. Erickson, **Christian Theology – 2nd Ed.**, (Baker Books, 1983)

* Millard J. Erickson, **Introducing Christian Doctrine – 2nd Ed.**, (Baker Academic, 2001)

* Gordon D. Fee & Douglas Stuart, **How to Read the Bible for all its Worth**, (Zondervan, 2003)

* Stanley J. Grenz & Roger E. Olson, **Who Needs Theology? An invitation to the study of God**, (InterVarsity Press, 1996)

* Stanley J. Grenz, **Theology for the Community of God**, (William B. Eerdmans, 1994)

* Larry, D. Hart, **Truth Aflame**, (Zondervan, 1999)

* C.S. Lewis, **Mere Christianity**, (Harper Collins, 2012)

* I.H. Marshall, **The Origin of New Testament Christology**, (Intervarsity Press, 1990)

* Alister McGrath, **Christian Theology: An Introduction**, (Blackwell Publishing, 2010)

* D. Moody, **The Word of Truth – A Summary of Christian Doctrine Based on Biblical Revelation**, (William B. Eerdmans, Publishing Co., 1981)

* Daniel Migliore, **Faith Seeking Understanding**, (William B. Eerdmans Publishing Co., 1991)

* Bruce Milne, **Know The Truth**, (Intervarsity Press, 2002)

* Alister McGrath, **Understanding Doctrine**, (Hodder & Stoughton, 1990)

* Henry C. Thiessen, **Lectures in Systematic Theology**, (William B. Eerdmans Publishing Company, 1979)

* A.W. Tozer, **The Pursuit of God – The Human Thirst for the Divine**, (Authentic Media, 2012)

Week¹

Introduction

**Session 1 –
What is Theology & Why Is It Important?**
Nature & Necessity of Theology
Methods of Studying Theology
The Three Foundations of Theology
Sources of Theology

Break

Session 2 – The Role of the Bible
The Wonder of the Bible
Nature of Revelation
Old Testament & New Testament Tests for Canonicity

Session 3 – Your Personal Theology

Homework – Theology & My Local Church

Session 1
What Is Theology? Why Is It Important?

Outcomes

* Understand what theology is and why it is important
* Recognise important methods and sources to study theology
* Understand that Spirit, Community and Scripture are the three foundations essential for theological formation

Session 2
The Role of the Bible

Outcomes

* Understand and explain how the Bible was written
* Understand the nature and purpose of the Bible
* Understand how the Bible came to be compiled
* Be certain of the Bible's authenticity

Session 3
Your Personal Theology

In a small group setting, share your responses to the following questions.
You may also like to write some of your answers down.

The objective of this exercise is to help you place where you are in your thinking about your faith.

Application 1

1. Discuss this statement, "Everyone is a theologian."
Do you agree or disagree and why? (What would you have said before tonight's session?)

_____

_____

_____

_____

_____

_____

2. Describe some areas of your daily life where your personal theology guides your decisions or actions.

_____

_____

_____

_____

_____

_____

_____

3. What are the risks involved (personally and for others) if we are missing one of the three foundations of theology? _Give examples._

_____

_____

_____

_____

_____

_____

_____

Application 2

1. What did you know about the way the Bible was written before this class? What in particular stuck out for you in the lesson about the Bible?

_____

_____

_____

_____

_____

2. 'No one has an excuse when it comes to a knowledge of God.' Is this a fair comment?

_____

_____

_____

_____

_____

3. Discuss the role of the Holy Spirit in the establishment of the scriptures? List ways in which the Holy Spirit helps us in our understanding of the scriptures.

_____

_____

_____

_____

_____

_____

_____

4. Discuss the statement, 'Don't simply read the bible, let the bible read you.'

_____

_____

_____

_____

_____

_____

_____

Homework

Theology & My Local Church

Log-on to your church's website and look for their Statement of Belief. Match the part of the statement that addresses each of the following areas:

The Bible _____

_____

_____

_____

_____

The Nature and Character of God _____

_____

_____

_____

_____

_____

The Reality of Sin _____

_____

_____

_____

_____

_____

The Nature of Jesus _____

_____

_____

_____

_____

Salvation _____

_____

_____

_____

_____

The Person and Work of the Holy Spirit _____

_____

_____

_____

_____

_____

The Church _____

_____

_____

_____

_____

_____

Our Purpose _____

_____

_____

_____

Week²

Introduction

Session 1 –
God – The Nature & Character of God (Part 1)
Importance of Knowing God
Attributes of God
How to Apply It

Break

Session 2 – God – Trinity (Part 1)
Trinity in Old Testament & New Testament
Biblical Evidence
Social Analogy of Trinity
Application of Trinity

Session 3 –
Understanding How the Doctrine of God
Impacts Our Lives.

Homework –
The Nature of God: In My Local Church

Session 1
Nature & Character of God (Part 1)

Outcomes

* To identify and describe the nature and character of God
* Recognise how our understanding of God impacts our daily Christian walk

---

Session 2
God – Trinity (Part 1)

Outcomes

* Identify God as one essence and three persons
* Identify scriptures in the Old and New Testament that refer to God as Triune
* Realise the implications of the doctrine for life and ministry

Session 3
Understanding how the doctrine of God Impacts our Lives

Discuss the following questions in a small group setting. You may like to write some of your group's answers down.

1. What do the terms Omnipotent, Omnipresent and Omniscient mean? Are these attributes of God's Greatness or his Goodness as described in the lecture?

2. How would you explain the Goodness of God? Identify some of the attributes of God's goodness, and select one attribute that brings forth a grateful response in your own heart.

_____

_____

_____

_____

_____

_____

_____

_____

3. Is the statement, 'the doctrine of the Trinity is fundamental to Christian theology' a valid comment? If so, why? Give the three simple statements which explain God's three-in-one nature.

_____

_____

_____

4. In your group, see if you can come up with a simple explanation of the Trinity. Remember this doctrine is central to our belief.

Homework

Practical Exercise

While attending the weekend services in your church, identify some references that are made regarding the attributes of God.

1. How are God's attributes demonstrated, praised and honoured?

_____

_____

_____

_____

_____

_____

_____

_____

2. Identify any references to God's attributes in the songs sung during the weekend service.

_____

_____

_____

_____

_____

_____

_____

_____

_____

_____

_____

_____

_____

_____

_____

3. Consider the implications of Trinity in your own life. Remember that an appropriate application as image-bearers of the Triune God means we are:

★ **Persons who know who they are** – and are not threatened by others
★ **Persons who know their function** – and submit them to eternal purpose
★ **Persons who co-exist and are united in love** – and not dependent because of need
★ **Persons who in-dwell & partake of one another** – and not out-perform or take from one another – just as Christ prayed in John 17:21, 'that all of them may be one, Father, just as you are in me and I am in you. May they also be in us so that the world may believe that you have sent me.'

Which of these can you see modelled in your own life? Which one would you like to see grow?
Write your own prayer to expresses this.

_____

_____

_____

_____

_____

_____

_____

_____

_____

_____

_____

_____

_____

_____

_____

_____

_____

_____

_____

_____

_____

On a Practical Note in Preparation for Next Week

Prepare your testimony, with particular reference to your recognition of your own need for salvation, and how the Holy Spirit met you individually. List the changes that have resulted as a since your conversion.

Week³

Introduction

Session 1 – Humanity
We are the Good Creation of God
Origin of Humanity
Created In The Image of God
Implications

Break

Session 2 – The Reality of Evil and Sin
Reality of Evil
Adam's Sin, All of Our Sin
Consequences of Sin
We Are the Object of God's Redemptive Activity

Session 3 –
Where I've Been is Not Where I'm Going

Homework – Humanity In Relation To Our Creator: In My Local Church

Session 1
Humanity

Session 2
The Reality of Evil & Sin

Outcomes

* Understand the theological teaching of the fall of humanity
* Recognise the nature, extent and effects of sin
* Identify sin's effects and realise that humanity and all of creation are the object of God's redemptive activity

Session 3
Where I've Been Is Not Where I'm Going

Discuss the following questions in a small group setting. You may like to write some of your group's answers down.

1. Share some of the varying challenges you have faced in regards to the effects of sin in your own life, and how you have overcome those. Use the categories given in the lesson, (relation to God, each other, ourselves, etc.)

_____

_____

_____

_____

_____

_____

_____

_____

2. Your group is probably made up of people with a range of different Christian backgrounds – some have grown up in the faith and others came to faith at a later stage in life. What do you notice is similar and different in each of your journeys?

_____

_____

_____

_____

_____

_____

3. In the lesson, we learned that sin affects our total being – our will, our thoughts, our emotions, and our behaviour. Pastor Brian Houston often says, 'No matter what happens in your life, never develop a wounded spirit.' What is the impact of ignoring this advice? And how do we 'guard our heart' practically?

_____

_____

_____

_____

_____

_____

4. How can your personal testimony impact your unsaved family, friends, peers, and work colleagues?

_____

_____

_____

_____

_____

_____

5. List the changes that have been evident in your life since beginning your walk with God.
Are there areas that you would like to see a personal victory in? Ask your group to pray for you.

_____

_____

_____

_____

_____

Practical Exercise

While attending the weekend services in church, identify some references that are made to humankind and our position in relation to our Creator at any point in the service.

1. How is the relationship between God and humanity defined or described?

_____

_____

_____

_____

_____

_____

_____

_____

_____

_____

_____

2. Identify any references to our humanity in these exerts from these two songs off of the Hillsong United Zion album. How do the lyrics describe humanity? What phrases impact you personally? Why?

Song 'Mercy Mercy' from Zion

Mercy mercy
Bring me to my knees
As the morning calls to light the dark in me

Heaven's story
Breathing life into my bones
Spirit lift me from this wasteland lead me home

Now I find my life in Yours
My eyes on Your Name
Arrest my heart from its reckless path
Release the chains in me

Awake my soul to the hope You hold
Your grace is all I need

Humble glory
Chose to carry all my shame
Rendered worthy in the shadow of Your Name

Gracious fury
Written in my Saviour's scars
Mercy mercy now engraved upon my heart

Song 'Tapestry' from Zion

Maker of earth and sky
And everything before our eyes
Your word formed life and light
Within the crucible of time
The genesis of all mankind

Our lives a tapestry of grace
Your hand has weaved together
In You no thread will ever fray
This hope is ours forever

Your work of art a mystery
Beyond all earthly measure
Your love for us a masterpiece
Jesus our hope always

3. Look at the following Scriptures and consider the implications of each. What does each one tell us about God and humanity?

Genesis 1:26   *Genesis 2:18*
Job 33:4   *Matthew 10:28*
Psalm 139:14   *1 Corinthians 11:11-12*
Matthew 19:4   *Philippians 3:20*

_____

_____

_____

_____

_____

_____

_____

_____

_____

_____

_____

_____

Q4. What is the significance of these to our daily Christian walk?

_____

_____

_____

_____

_____

_____

_____

_____

_____

_____

_____

_____

_____

_____

On a Practical Note

Consider this quotation from Selah 2, a book by Pastor Brian Houston:

"Salvation is more than an insurance policy against hell. Don't just live saved – live called."

Here Pastor Brian considers 2 Timothy 1:9 'God has saved us and called us with a holy calling…' What would be the indicators of a Christian living his/her life the way this quotation warns not to? What is the difference in your own life to living 'saved' and 'called'? Write down practical examples.

_____

_____

_____

_____

_____

_____

_____

_____

_____

_____

Homework

Humanity In Relation To Our Creator – In My Local Church

Character Study - Jesus

Take ten minutes to consider who Jesus is. Write down your initial thoughts. Some of your responses may be more doctrinal, while others might reflect a devotional perspective.

1. List two or three scriptures that confirm Jesus' divinity.

_____

_____

_____

_____

Perform the same exercise for Jesus' humanity.

_____

_____

_____

_____

2. What is the significance of Jesus being both human and divine?

_____

_____

_____

_____

_____

_____

3. Together read one of the gospel accounts of the death and resurrection of Jesus. (Matt 27:11-28:15; Mark 15:1-16:8; Luke 23:1-24:12; John 18:28-20:9) You may also compare differing gospel accounts. What were some of the emotions you experience as you read through the account?

_____

_____

_____

_____

_____

_____

_____

_____

_____

_____

4. How does the knowledge of Jesus' actions for you impact your everyday life? What areas of your life have been significantly altered as a result of this reality?

_____

_____

_____

_____

_____

_____

_____

Putting it into Practice

Can you think of any movies you have seen that cover the death and resurrection of Jesus? What has been the impact of these films on you personally?

_____

_____

_____

_____

_____

_____

_____

_____

_____

_____

_____

_____

_____

_____

_____

Week⁴

Introduction

Session 1 – Jesus – His Divinity & Humanity
Biblical Evidence
Significance of the Doctrine
Impact on our Faith Journey

Break

Session 2 –
Jesus: The Cross, Atonement & Resurrection
Why Was the Cross Necessary?
What Happened at the Cross?
Biblical Images of the Atonement
How should we respond?

Session 3 – The Time Was Right

Homework – Sharing the Good News

Session 1

Jesus – His Humanity & Divinity

Outcomes

* Provide evidence to support the humanity and divinity of Jesus Christ
* Explain why the humanity and divinity of Christ is important
* Identify the implications of Jesus being both human and divine

Session 2
Jesus – The Cross, Atonement & Resurrection

Outcomes
* Recognise the centrality of the cross to the Christian life
* Identify key biblical and theological images of the atonement
* Formulate a response to Christ's work

Session 3
The Time Was Right

1. Read Galatians 4:1-7 aloud as a group.
In the context of this passage, what was the purpose of Jesus' coming?

_____

_____

_____

_____

_____

_____

_____

_____

_____

_____

2. Read the following passages:

Matthew 28:19   *John 1:1-5*   *Acts 20:28*
Romans 9:5   *Titus 2:13*   *2 Peter 1:1*

_____

_____

_____

_____

_____

_____

_____

_____

_____

_____

Do these scriptures represent Jesus' humanity or divinity? Are there any specific aspects that are covered in these scriptures?

_____

_____

_____

_____

_____

_____

3. Read the following passages:

Matthew 1:25   *Hebrews 5:8*   *John 4:6*
Matthew 21:18   *Luke 10:21*   *John 11:5*

Which aspects of Jesus' humanity are evidenced by these verses?

_____

_____

_____

_____

_____

4. List the biblical and theological images of the atonement. In one sentence, write a definition of each of the biblical images.

_____

_____

_____

_____

_____

_____

5. As a group consider how you would share the gospel with a person who is not yet a Christian, by creatively presenting key aspects of the doctrine of the atonement. Record your ideas and nominate a spokesperson from your group to share what you come up with.

_____

_____

_____

_____

_____

_____

Homework

Sharing the Good News

Practical Exercise

Using the creative gospel presentation you created during the class, look for opportunities to share Jesus with an unsaved person in your world. It may be a family member, or a friend, a fellow student, or a work colleague.

1. Which aspect of this exercise was the most difficult? Was it the process of creating the evangelism strategy, or was it the delivery?

2. How did the person respond?

_____

_____

_____

_____

_____

_____

_____

3. Are there any aspects of the exercise that you would re-work to make the outreach more effective?

_____

_____

_____

_____

_____

Reflection

1. How have the doctrines we've covered in this subject so far begun to affect your understanding of the scriptures?

_____

_____

_____

_____

_____

_____

_____

_____

_____

2. How are the doctrines we've covered in this subject so far affecting how you walk with God?

_____

_____

3. How have the doctrines we've covered in this subject so far begun to affect how you serve and minister?

Week⁵

Introduction

Session 1 – Salvation & Blessing
What is Salvation?
What Are We Saved From? For?
Role of the Holy Spirit in Salvation

Break

Session 2 – Sanctification & the Spirit
What is Sanctification & How Is It Achieved?
What is the Role of the Holy Spirit In Sanctification?
Result of Transformation: Fruit of the Spirit

Session 3 – Walking With the Holy Spirit

Homework – Divinely Empowered

Session 1
Salvation & Blessing

Outcomes

* Understand what salvation is
* Understand that salvation is a process
* Explain the role of the Holy Spirit in the believer's conversion
* Actively participate in the faith community

Session 2
Sanctification & the Spirit

Outcomes

* Explain the meaning of sanctification
* Identify the role of the Holy Spirit and the role of the believer in sanctification
* Take responsibility for individual sanctification by cooperating with the Holy Spirit

Session 3
Walking with the Holy Spirit

1. Read this verse aloud together:

"For those who are led by the Spirit of God are the children of God. The Spirit you received does not make you slaves, so that you live in fear again; rather, the Spirit you received brought about your adoption to sonship. And by him we cry, "Abba, Father." The Spirit himself testifies with our spirit that we are God's children. Now if we are children, then we are heirs—heirs of God and co-heirs with Christ, if indeed we share in his sufferings in order that we may also share in his glory." (Romans 8:14-17)

How might the truth of this passage better help you walk with the Holy Spirit? Which portion jumps out to you and why?

_____

_____

_____

_____

_____

_____

_____

2. Explain sanctification in your own words.

_____

_____

_____

_____

_____

3. What is the Holy Spirit's role in the process of sanctification? Compare and contrast your own responsibility and the Holy Spirit's responsibility.

_____

_____

_____

_____

_____

_____

_____

_____

4. How would your life be different if the fruit of the Spirit were more prominent and practiced in your life?

_____

_____

_____

_____

_____

_____

_____

_____

_____

_____

_____

_____

5. Which of the fruit of the Holy Spirit do you believe could grow in your life?
Pray as a group that God will help develop this.

_____

_____

_____

_____

_____

_____

_____

_____

_____

_____

_____

Homework

Read Acts 1:4-8 and Acts 2:1-13.

1. Why was the Holy Spirit given to the believers?

_____

_____

_____

_____

2. What does the passage tell us about how we should fulfil our commission?

_____

_____

_____

3. What are the manifestations of the power of the Holy Spirit in the lives of the New Testament believers?

_____

_____

_____

_____

_____

_____

_____

_____

4. What effect did the empowerment of the Holy Spirit have upon the believers?

_____

_____

_____

_____

_____

5. What are the manifestations of the power of the Spirit in your life?

_____

_____

_____

_____

_____

_____

_____

_____

_____

_____

_____

6. Do you ever find yourself trying to do things on/in your own power? What has been the result of this?

Week⁶

Introduction

**Session 1 –
Sanctification & Spirit: Gifts of the Spirit**
Baptism of the Holy Spirit
How to Be Filled With the Holy Spirit
What Happens When I Am Filled With the Holy Spirit?
Gifts

Break

Session 2 – Church as a Community
Who Is the Church?
Biblical Images of the Church

Session 3 – You & the Church Community

Homework – Divinely Empowered

Session 1
Sanctification & Spirit – Gifts & Power

Outcomes
* Understand the gifts of the Holy Spirit
* Identify the different kinds and functions of the gifts

Session 2
Church – Church as a Community

Outcomes

* ★ Understand who the Church is
* ★ Understand that the Church is a community
* ★ Identify ways to integrate themselves into the community

Session 3
You & The Church Community

Our conversion involves our incorporation into the community of Christ.

1. What is God trying to achieve with the Church as a Community? Why is it important to Him? Identify some relevant scriptures.

_____

_____

_____

_____

_____

_____

_____

_____

_____

2. In your life, what has been the result of being part of this community?

_____

_____

_____

_____

_____

_____

3. How does your local church incorporate believers into the community?

_____

_____

_____

_____

_____

_____

4. What steps can you take to better integrate yourself into the community?

_____

_____

_____

_____

_____

_____

_____

5. What steps can you take to help new believers integrate into the community?

_____

_____

_____

_____

_____

Homework

1. *'The church, you see, is not peripheral to the world; the world is peripheral to the church. The church is Christ's body, in which he speaks and acts, by which he fills everything with his presence'* (Ephesians 1:23 MSG)

a. What does this passage tell us about God's intentions for the church? Can you think of other relevant scriptures?

_____

_____

_____

_____

b. What does this passage tell us about the relationship with and mission of the church to the world?

_____

_____

_____

_____

_____

_____

2. What is the mission statement of your local church? Check your church website to get the information.

_____

_____

_____

_____

_____

_____

3. How is this mission outworked in your church?

_____

_____

_____

_____

_____

_____

_____

4. As a member of your local church, how do you personally demonstrate this mission in your life?

a. Read Luke 24:45-49, Matthew 28:18-20, Mark 16:15-18 and Acts 1:8. What do these passages tell us about the extent of the mission of the church?

_____

_____

_____

_____

_____

_____

b. One need not move or go overseas to fulfil the Great Commission. It can be done within our own very backyard. What would you consider the 'all nations', 'all creation', 'Jerusalem', 'Judea', 'Samaria' and the 'remotest part of the earth' for you?

_____

_____

_____

_____

_____

_____

_____

c. How can you fulfil the Great Commission in your own backyard? Identify one thing that you will do for the next seven days in response to the Great Commission?

_____

_____

_____

_____

_____

_____

6. Read Matthew 24:1-28. What does the passage tell us about the condition of the world prior to the coming of Jesus and the end of the age?

_____

_____

_____

_____

_____

_____

7. Jesus gave some specific words of instruction regarding the last times. What are these instructions in terms of the following:

a. When he is coming. (Read Matthew 24:32-41)

_____

_____

_____

_____

_____

_____

_____

_____

b. How we are to recognise the season of his return. (Read Matthew 24:37-39 and Genesis 7:12-17)

_____

_____

_____

_____

_____

_____

_____

c. What we need to do while waiting for his return. (Read Matthew 24:42-51 and Matthew 25:1-30)

_____

_____

_____

_____

_____

_____

_____

Week⁷

Introduction

Session 1 – The Church & Its Mission
For the Praise of His Glory
Mission & Purpose of the Church

Break

Session 2 – Resurrection & Return:
The Completion of God's Plan
The Resurrection & Second Coming of Christ
Eschatology: Kingdom of God
Hope

Session 3 – Blessed in Every Way

Next Steps & Closing

Session 1
The Church & It's Mission

Outcomes

* Understand the key markers relating to the Church
* Identify key scriptures that detail the Church and its mission
* Recognise individuals' role in the Church and its mission

Session 2

Resurrection & Return –
The Completion of God's Plan

Outcomes

* Explain that eschatology is about hope and the kingdom of God
* Discuss the importance of the resurrection of Jesus Christ and principles to understanding his second coming
* Examine the kingdom of God and its relevance in the life of every believer

Session 3
Blessed in Every Way

Exercise 1

Review Questions 6 and 7 from last week's homework.
Take the time to read through the Scriptures listed and discuss openly in the group.

Exercise 2

The following questions are designed to make the lecture material practical. Give some thought to the questions and share your outcomes amongst yourselves.

1. How are you preparing yourself for the return of Jesus?

_____

_____

_____

_____

_____

_____

2. What kind of attitude should we have about the last days?

_____

_____

_____

_____

_____

3. How should the reality of 'the now and not yet' affect how we pray? How we live?

_____

_____

_____

_____

_____

_____

_____

_____